Rob Versus The Scammers

Protecting The World Against Fraud,
Nuisance Calls & Downright Phony Scams.

Rob Anspach

Rob Versus The Scammers
Protecting The World Against Fraud, Nuisance Calls
& Downright Phony Scams.

ISBN 10: 1-7324682-2-2
ISBN 13: 978-1-7324682-2-1

Printed in USA

Disclaimer: Oh yes, we must have a disclaimer…it makes the lawyers happy. So, if you are to take on the scammers like the author has in this book, please understand that if you do, you may start getting more calls, more texts and more emails. Also most scammers use fake names, sometimes even celebrity names or names from people on television shows and movies. So use the resources mentioned in the book as a guide to help you avoid becoming the victim of a scam.

Table of Contents

WARNING:Criminal Investigation Division of I.R.S is filing a lawsuit against you, for more information call on +1-2025808292 on urgent basis otherwise your arrest warrant will be forwarded to your local police department and your property and bank accounts and social benefits will be frozen by government.

What People Are Saying

"Rob Anspach has written what can only be considered a social primer for dealing effectively with phone scammers while at the same time thoroughly enjoying yourself at their expense. Not so very long ago I did what I considered to be the 'right thing' by adding my cell phone to the government DO NOT CALL list. I know, I know, what was I thinking? Before making that fatal mistake when my phone rang I knew it was only one of a handful of people who actually have my number.
Then...the calls began. And they kept coming.
It got so bad that I had to turn the ringer off on my phone and even considered getting a new number. Rob to the rescue! He began sharing his hilarious dialogues with these scammers on Facebook and I got to where I went looking for them each day and was actively disappointed when there was nothing new. I even copied some into scripts of a sort and began using them against our shared mortal enemies. If you feel the need to say hello when your phone rings, have this primer ready!"
– Denise Griffitts, Your Office On The Web

"And yet again Mr. Anspach has written another amazing book. This time putting together humor and learning. Read and find out not only what scams are in the world so you are not a victim but know you have a trusted professional who is busting up scams while making people laugh." - **Paul David Carpenter**

"Rob Anspach is a really good person. How could he *not* be, with so many rich dead foreigners wishing to share their fortunes with him? For anyone who has been scammed, flimflammed or bamboozled, this book serves as a screening service to help avoid future loss of finances, security or sanity. Think of Rob Anspach as Scammer TSA...and he's wearing an extra-large rubber glove." - **Steve Gamlin, Keynote Speaker/Author, The Motivational Firewood™ Guy**

"Rob Anspach has taken the calls, gotten the emails and the texts to prove it's not all real out there people. Rob seriously pokes fun at the unsuspecting scammers and gives them a taste of their own medicine. "Rob Versus The Scammers" is hilarious and a book everyone needs to read, not to make you skeptical (ok, maybe a little), but to keep you on your toes. Thanks for writing this Rob Anspach. There were a few shocking surprises in there for me, but more importantly you've included the call to actions people need to take so they can combat this nonsense." - **Laura Toogood**

"Ha-ha Rob, you're so funny and I love that you waste the time of the scammers so they have less time to scam other more vulnerable people! I do so enjoy reading how you do this and am always amazed by the things you say to them and so fast too. In this book Rob not only provides the words we all wish we could think of when these people call us, but also how to stay safe from scams and where to report them. Overall, a light entertaining read that will have you in admiration of his quick wit and one-man mission to rob the scammers of time and patience!"
- **Cémanthe McKenzie, Managing Director, New Media Angels Ltd. (United Kingdom)**

"Although it may seem like a sideshow topic to some, the very fact that scammers persist in targeting people through increasingly sophisticated schemes shows it continues to be an effective and lucrative criminal enterprise. Highly intelligent people I know personally have either been conned out of their money, or so frightened by the scammers they actually thought about sending the money and felt the need to ask someone. Fortunately for all of us, Rob Anspach is on the case. He has delivered an entertaining, and at the same time invaluable, cautionary tale that we all need to read. Believe me, this is worth your time."
–**Adam Hommey, Speaker • Author • Consultant • Trainer www.AdamHommey.com**

"If you want to take your personal frustration with the many scammers of the world pestering you and do something fun with it, I highly recommend this entertaining book to give you the strategies to deal with all the phony fraud scams. I guarantee this book will give you the "materials and scripts you need to deal with all the Nuisance calls and scams and have fun doing it." - **Lee Milteer, Author of "Success Is an Inside Job" www.LeeMilteer.com**

"If you follow Rob on Facebook you have most likely been regaled with an odd tale or two of how Rob will intentionally mess with scammers, waste their time to prevent them from scamming the masses. If you haven't, then this is your opportunity to laugh, roll your eyes, and jump into a scammer's worst nightmare as Rob leads them down one rabbit trail after another leaving them bewildered and pissed off. It is a quick fun read, with valuable lessons on how you can protect yourself, your bank account as well as your credit. I give this book a five letter recommendation. Buy It." – **Paul Douglas, Titan Marketing Solutions (Winnipeg, Canada) & Co-Author of "Optimize This"**

INTRODUCTION
By: Rob Anspach

Over the last few years the amount of nuisance calls, texts and emails have increased exponentially. Scammers know it's a numbers game. The more people they contact the better chance they will have at winning the scam.

Well, for me…that's not going to work. I don't play their game. And so, I fight back. Armed with sarcasm, wit and a dash of meanness…I embark on my battles.

I use various phone apps that give me a heads up on who's calling. I can either ignore the call or answer it. If I answer, I try to keep the scammers on the line as long as possible and waste their time. Sure, some might argue that I'm wasting my time, or that I'm poking a hornet's nest, but then you wouldn't be reading about my adventures in a book would you?

Years ago, the "Do Not Call" lists were created to help consumers keep their phones clear of these unsolicited calls. You would call a special number or go to a website and then enter your information and upon doing so, the amount of telemarketing calls you received were supposed to stop or be considerably reduced.

Well, we all know how great that system worked. And don't get me started on the multitude of texts and emails now invading my inbox and mobile with offers, notices, warnings, jobs I never applied for, lotteries I never entered and long lost relatives leaving me millions.

So these are my adventures fighting the scammers. On the phone, via text and through email…I make a point to string them along, frustrate them and be the proverbial thorn in their side.

I've also included a few other scams you might come across such as the Microsoft Blue Screen Warning, the Bitcoin Email scam, IRS scam and the "Do You Accept Credit Cards" text scam.

Enjoy the book, and stay safe.

Rob Anspach

www.AnspachMedia.com

Rob Versus The Scammers

CHAPTER 1

Card Services

These guys are the worst, I hate them. So, when they call, I make it
a point to screw with them and waste their time.

I Never Did Get My Cappuccino

Me: Hey!

Caller: I see you pressed one to get the lower interest.

Me: Nah, I pressed 5 to order a cappuccino.

Caller: Sir, we are here to save you thousands on your interest, all I need is your credit card information.

Me: Oh, so no cappuccino then?

Caller: Can you give me your credit card information?

Me: Yes, which one.

Caller: The card with the highest balance.

Me: Well do you want the one with the highest balance or the one with the highest interest?

Caller: Just give me the card number.

Me: Aren't we a tad rude.

Caller: Sir, this process would go so much smoother if you cooperated.

Me: Ah yes, it's my fault is it?

Caller: Sir, I'm trying to be patient with you.

Me: Well, you're failing at it.

Caller: Do you want the lower interest rate or not?

Me: I really want a cappuccino - can you help me with that?

Caller: Sir you are wasting my time.

Me: Time is relative...for you it might be a waste, for me it's providing much entertainment.

Caller: Sir just please read off the card numbers.

Me: Where are you located?

Caller: New York

Me: Where in New York?

Caller: New York City

Me: What's the street address?

Caller: Sir why all the questions?

Me: Because I don't give out my digits to every caller who says they can help me. I need to know this isn't a scam.

Caller: I assure you Sir, your card numbers are only used to pull up your information and give you the best deal.

Me: Yes, but all that information should already be at your disposal.

Caller: Sir we represent all the banks.

Me: I don't use a bank...I use a credit union.

Caller: All the banks we do.

Me: You said your calling from New York, so why does your number appearing on my caller ID say Tennessee?

Caller: We route our calls through call centers all over.

Me: Even Pakistan?

Caller: Yes

Me: Gotcha!

Caller hung up.

NOTE: In most cases, the callers that perpetrate this scam are housed in crowded call centers outside the reaches of the United States, Canada & British law enforcement. They utilize technology to mask and spoof caller ID's. But, it's usually their heavy accents and broken English that gives them away.

From 1800-945-2000 Chase Card (NOT)

Me: Hello!

Caller: This is Card Services.

Me: The number comes up as Chase - are you Card Services or Chase?

Caller: Sir we are Card Services representing Chase, Citi, Bank of America, Visa and MasterCard.

Me: What do you want?

Caller: We want to give you a lower interest rate.

Me: Great let's have it.

Caller: Can you tell me the last 4 digits of your highest balance card?

Me: No!

Caller: And why not?

Me: Because I think we should play a game.

Caller: What are the last 4 digits?

Me: Yes that's the game...guess the digits.

Caller: No sir just tell me the numbers.

Me: Oh don't be a stick in the mud, guess.

Caller hung up

NOTE: Card Services is not affiliated with any legitimate Credit Card Company. And, in most cases they have no idea who they are calling. But the moment you give them your real information is when they rip you off. I have received calls where the scammer has spoofed the caller ID of the actual credit card company. The moment they start asking for your information just hang up, or fight back and completely waste their time.

Call from +1 (797)966

You just know it's a scammer when the caller ID is missing numbers. So why not play along.

Me: Yo, what ya want?

Caller: This is Card Services offering you a lower interest on your credit cards.

Me: Sorry, I beat you to it.

Caller: Sir?

Me: I just broke into this home, tied the owners up and stole their credit cards, jewelry and car keys. Oh and I'm taking their phones too.

Caller: So they won't be able to receive calls?

Me: Nope.

Caller hung up.

NOTE: The use of Nomorobo (or similar) call screening technology will end these nuisance calls (see resources in back of book).

Card Services are calling me again...

...you'd think they would learn by now.

So I played along as usual.

Gave them false information and they tried to verify it...and what do you know...nothing matched.

Caller: Sir, can please read the entire card number - all 16 digits.

Me: Sure.

Caller: Sir, aloud please.

Me: Oh, I'm sorry. You weren't very clear. {So I make up 16 numbers.}

Caller: Sir, can you verify your zip code?

Me: Do you mean the zip code I'm in now or the zip code where the card statement goes to?

Caller: Sir, where the card statement goes to.

Me: Got it...okay 90210

Sir, are you sure that is the right zip code?

Me: I'm pretty sure, yeah.

Caller: Sir, nothing is matching. Is the card in your name?

Me: No it isn't.

Caller: Sir, what do you mean no it isn't?

Me: Well, you didn't ask my name, you only asked for a card number.

Caller: Sir, do you want a lower rate or not?

Me: Well I'm thinking the guy that owns this card might since you're going to scam him of his money.

{Calls me a mother-f'er and hangs up.}

NOTE: These scammers have no real ability to grant you a lower rate. But they will gladly take your credit card information and make themselves and the call center they work for richer. So if you're going to take their call, string them along, keep them on the phone and have fun with them.

Mr. Scammer Needs A Nap

Another day, another Card Services scammer.

Caller 1: Hello is this Mr. Stafford?

{I didn't want to acknowledge who I really was, so I answered...}

Me: Why yes it is.

{Unfortunately the person calling me sounded like he hasn't slept in 3 days. Every other word he paused to yawn.}

Me: Does the little scammer need a nap?
{I seriously thought the call would end right then...but nope}

Caller 1: Yes, Sir I sure do.

Me: Okay put someone else on the line who can help me so you can take a nap.

Caller 2: Sir, please excuse my associate, I will help you now.

Me: Awesome I have lots of cards that need a lower interest rate.

{Gave them fictitious card numbers, expiration dates and zip codes - was put on hold for 5 minutes}

Caller 2: Sir, the number you gave is from a US Bank card is that correct.

Me: Sure is. I'm really anxious to get a lower rate.

Caller 2: Okay give me a few minutes to get things going

{on hold for 6 more minutes}

Caller 2: Sir your information doesn't seem to match

Me: Oh really.

Caller 2: Can you read the numbers back to me again.

{Supplied him with the fake information all over again - waited another 6 more minutes for him to investigate}

Caller 2: Sir, are you still using those cards?

Me: No I haven't used them in some time.

Caller 2: But do you make payments to them?

Me: No I haven't made payments to them either.

Caller 2: What do you mean?

Me: Are we going to do this deal or not?

Caller 2: Okay Sir let me check a 3rd time.

Me: Yes, please check again.

{Another 5 minutes goes by}

Caller 2: I just don't know what is going on Sir.

Me: Oh, I know what's going on. I just wasted 26 minutes of your time. That was fun. Can we do it again tomorrow?

Caller 2: F-You.
{hangs up}

NOTE: Most of these call centers originate in foreign lands and they may have 40-50 people working in a crowded call center 12-16 hours a day. If they can scam one person an hour they are doing well. Don't let it be you. Fight back.

CHAPTER 2

Electric Rate Scammers

Honing their skills so one day they too can be a
Card Services scammer.

This is Po-to-mac Edison calling about your electric.

Me: Po-to-mac Edison you say?

Caller: Yes Po-to-mac Edison…we are letting you know your electric will be shut off in 45 minutes if you don't agree to pay today.

Me: Oh, okay…just shut it off then.

Caller: Sir, we are serious. If you don't pay immediately your electric will be shut off.

Me: Good…shut it off!

Caller: We are scheduled to shut it off today.

Me: Today? I thought you said 45 minutes.

Caller: Sir, I don't think you understand the situation. We will shut off your electric.

Me: Yes, I understand. Please send the guy over and disconnect the electric.

Caller: Do you have a Walgreens nearby?

Me: A Walgreens?

Caller: Yes, sir…can you get to a Walgreens and then I'll tell how to proceed to pay us.

Me: Nah, send your guy over and shut off the electric.

Caller: Sir, if you go to Walgreens we can prevent your electric from being shut off.

Me: Nah, I want to see your technician get here in the next 45 minutes…because that's one hell of a drive considering I'm about 100 miles away and not served by Potomac Edison and don't fall for stupid scams like this.

The caller told me to 'F" off and I shouldn't waste his precious time, then he hung up.

NOTE: Deregulation of the electric industry allowed consumers more choice in selecting who they use for their electric supplier. This created an opportunity for scammers to use "bait and switch" tactics to lure people into giving out their information. If the caller doesn't represent your electric supplier, either hang up, or completely waste their time.

That call was electrifying...sort of.

Caller: Good morning Sir, we would like to offer you a lower rate on your PECO Energy service.

Me: Really, how so?

Caller: Well, Sir if you can grab a pencil and piece of paper I will review and you can take notes.

Me: What decade are we in... I can just jot the notes in my phone as we speak.

Caller: Hmm, okay Sir...next I will need a copy of your PECO Energy invoice so we can compare rates.

Me: That might be a problem.

Caller: Sir, why is that?

Me: Well I don't get an invoice.

Caller: What do you mean you don't get an invoice.

Me: PECO Energy doesn't send me an invoice

Caller: Why is that Sir?

Me: Because I'm not a customer of PECO Energy.

Caller: Wow, our records say that you are.

Me: Well, I've never been.

Caller: Sir, I'm sure we can help you.

Me: With?

Caller: Lowering the rates with your current supplier.

Me: I doubt it.

Caller: Sir, can you tell us who your electric supplier is.

Me: I could, but first what is the rate you can give me.

Caller: I can't reveal that until you give us the name of your service.

Me: So basically you want me to give you information first before you share information with me, is that what I'm hearing?

Caller: Sir, we need to know who you are using before we can give you a rate.

Me: Well let's play a game...for every question you get right I will answer one question about me, okay? You ready to play?

Caller: Sir that is not how it works?

Me: Okay, here's my first question...ready? Are you from India or Pakistan?

{click} Caller hung up

NOTE: Be very careful when discussing your electric service with anyone that is not your current supplier. And if the caller asks questions that require you to say "YES" hang up immediately. They can use your "YES" as a way to transfer your electric service into a contract that may cost thousands of dollars to get out of.

This Was A Heavy Call.

Me: Hello!

Caller: Hi Sir, we are with SFE Energy calling to give you a lower wate.

Me: Yes, I would like to lower my weight.

Caller: Sir let me transfer to the Wate Supervisor.

Me: A Weight Supervisor?

Caller: Yes, Sir, a Wate Supervisor.

Me: So how is a supervisor going to lower my weight?

Wate Supervisor: Hi Sir I will be taking over the call.

Me: So you are the weight supervisor?

Wate Supervisor: Yes, Sir I will need a copy of your electric bill to lower your wate.

Me: What the heck does my electric bill have to do with lowering my weight?

Wate Supervisor: Sir by analyzing your electric bill we can offer you a lower wate.

Me: I'm confused is this like weight watchers or something?

Wate Supervisor: Sir this is about your electric bill, not weight watchers.

Me: Will I need weight reduction surgery then?

Wate Supervisor: Sir, I have no idea what you are talking about.

Me: You are the weight supervisor aren't you?

Wate Supervisor: Sir, it's your electric wate.

Me: I have no idea electric weighed anything.
   {He hung up}

I knew he meant RATE, but I just didn't want to give him the satisfaction.

NOTE: If one person calls you then after a minute or so the call is transferred to another person, it's usually a scam.

Rob Anspach

My Mobile Phone Rings:

(the Hiya phone app tells me it's a telemarketer so I figured I would answer and have some fun.)

Caller: Sir what is your account number?

Me: Account for what?

Caller: Your electric account.

Me: No idea, not something I know by heart.

Caller: I can wait while you look.
{wasted 5 minutes walking up and down the stairs, let the dog out, poured some iced tea}

Me: Hmm couldn't find it, but I think it's online.

Caller: Okay I'll wait.

Me: What was I doing?

Caller: Looking for the account number.

Me: Oh yes, I logged into my account.

Caller: Sir can you read me the account number?

Me: Sure but first can you tell me the rate you are offering.

Caller: {rattles off some number}

Me: My current rate is lower than that.

Second Caller: Sir?

Me: Yes!

Second Caller: Sir, how can I help you?

Me: Where'd the other guy go?

Second Caller: He's new and I thought it best if I took over the call.

Me: Oh, you're better at the script, eh?

Second Caller: Sir what is the name of your supplier?

Me: George!

Second Caller: Sir, what?

Me: George!

Second Caller: That name is not on the list of electrical suppliers

Me: Oh, I thought you meant my drug supplier.
{They hung up}

CHAPTER 3

IRS Lawsuit Scam

The IRS does not text people…ever!

Text I received:

WARNING: Criminal Investigation Division of I.R.S is filing a lawsuit against you, for more information call on +1-2025808292 on urgent basis otherwise your arrest warrant will be forwarded to your local police department and your property and bank accounts and social benefits will be frozen by government.

So I texted back: My social benefits will be frozen? Say it isn't so.

Received: Please call the number.

Me: It's a Sunday, can't it wait until tomorrow?

Received: No, call the number.

Me: I'm busy.

Received: We are notifying the police.

Me: Okay, let me know when they are on their way.

Received: Please take this serious.

Me: Okay, I'm seriously turning on the outside light waiting for them.

Received: We can stop them from visiting you if you agree to take care of your IRS matter tonight.

Me: I bet you want money don't you?

Received: You owe $2654.59

Me: And I bet you want me to pay with Western Union or a gift card of some sort.

Received: Yes, that's right.

Me: Well will you accept a $29 Starbucks Card and a $63 Olive Garden card instead?

Received: Police are on the way.

Me: Awesome.

Received: F¥€k 0££

Me: I take it this isn't the IRS then.

~ no response ~

NOTE: The Internal Revenue Service will never text or call you. They don't accept payment through gift cards or Western Union and they won't notify the police to come after you. If you get a call or a text from the IRS simply ignore, delete or play along. Just don't give them your information.

Rob Versus The Scammers

CHAPTER 4

May I Have Your Name, Please?

Scammers rarely know your name when calling, so don't volunteer
the information to them.

"Hello is Anne there?"

Me: What? I think you have the wrong number.

Caller: Oh, okay well maybe you can help me then.

Me: Doubt it.

Caller: We are calling on behalf of the disabled veterans.

Me: Which ones?

Caller: Our national center is out of Colorado.

Me: Seems legit then, since you are calling me from a Pennsylvania number.

Caller: Can we count on you for a donation of $20?

Me: How much did you give?

Caller: I don't understand the question.

Me: If you want me to donate $20, how much did you donate?

Caller: We can take your credit card over the phone if you want to donate.

Me: Sure!

Caller: Is the card under your name "Anne"

Me: Yeah, that's right.

Caller: You don't sound like an Anne to me.

Me: Have I questioned your life choices?

Caller: I don't think you're going to help us, and you wasted my time.

<click>

I told him up front I doubt I could help him…I don't understand why he got pissy with me.

NOTE: I have gotten many of these so-called "wrong numbers" and they all seem to start off the same. This is the scammers way of testing the line to see if a real person picks up. And they always seem to use some vague charity for the reason why they are calling. Don't fall it. Ask lots of questions.

I'm the call center's worst nightmare!

Call taker: May I have your name please?

Me: What's wrong with your name?

Call taker: Sir, can you give me your name?

Me: Well, my parents gave me this name, I think they would be upset if I gave it away.

Call taker: Sir, please spell your name.

Me: R-O-B-E-R-T

Call taker: Sir, can you please slow down

Me: R---O---B---E---R---T

Call taker: Sir I'm not an idiot.

Me: R O B E R T okay

Call taker: Can you repeat that?

Me: I said it 3 freaking bloody times: slow, slower and regular.

Call taker: Okay Sir last name now.

Me: I don't think I have enough patience to go through that process again.

Call taker: Sir, we need that information to proceed

Me: You can go on without me.

Call taker: Hang on sir.

Me: For what?

{another voice comes on}

Call taker 2: Sir I would be glad to help you.

Me: Oh goody!

Call taker 2: May I have your name please?

Me: Oh we're playing this game again. Nope, not today. I'm out.

NOTE: If the caller doesn't understand plain English or how to spell common names, they are either dumber than a bag of wet rocks or they are scammers.

Please hold the line for a very important message...

Now you can be pain free with our patented brace system, to learn more press 9 now.

Call taker: Hi this is...Ja – Albert.

Me: Your name is Ja-Albert?

Call taker: No just Albert.

Me: Kind of like "Just Jack"?

Call taker: No... it's just Albert not Jack.

Me: So, just Albert not Jack...what's this all about?

Call taker: My name is just Albert!

Me: Yes, I think we already established that.

Call taker: My name is Albert!

Me: Why didn't you just say that instead of Ja-Albert?

Call taker: Mmm

Me: Is Albert even your real name?

{click} I guess I will never know.

CHAPTER 5

Home & Health Scams

You would think being less rude would help them, nope!

Call from 1(223)333-6944

Caller: Do you suffer from chronic pain?

{Hah, these callers have no idea who they are dealing with.}

Me: Yes, I suffer from pain.

Caller: Where do you suffer pain?

Me: In my neck, ears and butt.

Caller: Wow, you are in pain.

Me: Yep, holding the phone up answering these calls is making my neck hurt, your words are making my ears bleed and seriously these nuisance calls are a pain in my ass.

Caller: Do you have insurance?

Me: Yup.

Caller: How old are you?

Me: Why, are you hitting on me?

They hung up.

NOTE: Handing out your insurance information to strangers is a good way to lose it...permanently.

Hi Sir this is Cindy at American Financial Center calling to see if you need more money?

Me: Well Cindy I'm glad you called.

Cindy: We help Americans like you keep more of the money they earn.

Me: Well that's nice

Cindy: Sir, do you work?

Me: Well, you can say that.

Cindy: What is it that you do Sir?

Me: I rob banks for a living.

Cindy: Well Sir, that's nice, we can help you save the money you earn at your bank job.

Me: Really, wow, so you gonna help me launder the money then?

Cindy: Sir, I'm not certain what you said.

Me: Oh, I think you heard me...I rob banks and I need you to launder the money okay.

Cindy: Sir, do you owe money to any credit cards?

Me: Well, do you mean my own credit cards or the money that I charge to other people's cards?

Cindy: Sir how much total do you think you owe?

Me: Oh, from all the cards I scammed from people all over the globe about 5 million

Cindy: Is that on one or more cards?

Me: Oh, about 300 of them

Cindy: Do you know the interest you are paying?

Me: Zero

Cindy: Well Sir, I don't think you really need our service

Me: What gave it away?

<click>

NOTE: Most of these scammers have a tight script they stick to. If they don't understand what you're saying, they just ignore it and move on. Ask them lots of questions. The sillier the better. Get them off script and that's when the fun happens.

Sir, we are an organization dis-trib-but-ting sanitary napkins to schools in Somalia and India.

Me: Okay and?

Caller: Do you understand the situation?

Me: I don't even understand this call.
{They hung up}

A part of me really wants to know more about this sanitary napkin situation - sadly they called on an unknown number and I can't call back.

Now I may never know how this scam works.

NOTE: Some have told me they think this is a legitimate service. Maybe. But, when you screen as many calls, emails and texts as I do, you start to pick up on the common parlance of the scam. If you don't know the organization, don't give them your credit card information. Ever.

Sir, we are a Home Improvement Company offering all kinds of repairs like roofing, gutters, windows, doors and plumbing.

{background noise was filled with at least a dozen callers running through the same script}

Me: Hmm, could you repeat that, all the noise in the background is distracting.

Caller: Sir, we are a Home Improvement Company offering all kinds of repairs like roofing, gutters, windows, doors and plumbing.

Me: What did you say your company's name is?

Caller: Home Improvement Company!

Me: Hmm, never heard of you, what is it you do?

Caller: All kinds of home repairs like roof, gutters, windows, doors and plumbing.

Me: Do you offer electrical?
Caller: Yes!

Me: Do you offer siding replacement?

Caller: Yes!

Me: Do you offer dog poo yard clean up?

Caller: Sir, you name it we can fix it.

Me: Okay, I can probably come up with a list of repairs you can MacGyver.

Caller: Do you own your home?

Me: I pay a mortgage - which means I will probably be dead before it's paid for.

Caller: So in the future which repairs do you think you will need done to your home?

Me: It's a home...everything will need repaired at some point.

Caller: May we send someone out tomorrow to give you a quote?

Me: Where did you say you are located?

{Caller then botches the name of my town}

Me: So if you're local to my area how come you can't even pronounce the town's name correctly?

Caller: I'm new to the company.

Me: So you work for a company that has no real name in a town you can't pronounce

{caller doesn't even acknowledge my question and stays on script}

Caller: So tomorrow doesn't work, how about the next day?

Me: You're a pushy SOB aren't you?

Caller: Sir, we are just trying to make an appointment with you.

Me: To do what?

Caller: Give you a quote for repairs.

Me: Well you asked if I needed repairs in the future, not if I needed repairs right now.

Caller: But Sir we are in your area all this week.

Me: Well the number you called in on is not a local number.

Caller: We are calling from our national call center and we make thousands of calls a day all over the USA

Me: Wow, sounds like you have this scam down then.

Caller: Yes, Sir.

Me: So you admit it?

{Caller hung up}

NOTE: If you need home improvements your best recourse is to ask a neighbor, friend or colleague for a referral. They will tell you who they used and what the outcome was. Sure there are legitimate resources who do still use the phone to market themselves, however they usually call on a local number, pronounce the name of the town correctly and don't solicit all over the country for work.

Rob Versus The Scammers

CHAPTER 6

Press 1 To Get Scammed Again

Because pressing any other number isn't really an option.

Phone rings... it's a robotic voice telling me to press 1 for Card Services.

So I did.

As soon as a live person picks up...I quickly say...
"This is Rob from Card Services, how can I help you?"

Caller: Huh, what, this is Card Services, how can I help you?

Me: Would you like a lower interest rate on your card balances? I can help you with that, I just need to know the card with the highest balance, can you share that card with me.

Caller: Mmm, errr.

Me: Look sir, do you want the deal or not, all I need is your card number, the 3-digit code on the back and we can make this happen. Let's do it.

Caller: I think I have the wrong number.

Me: No you don't, you called me remember. So let's do this deal...give me those digits and read that card off to me...come on...I don't have all day. DO IT! DO IT! DO IT NOW!

Caller: Uh, um, well...

Me: Dude, are we doing this or not. Because so far you wasted 3 minutes of my time with your indecision, grow a back bone...read the card off to me now.

I hear him talking to another person, then Caller 2 gets on the line.

Caller 2: Sir who is this?

Me: It's Card Services and your buddy was going to give me his credit card number.

Caller 2: Sir, we are Card Services.

Me: Doubtful...you're not aggressive enough.

Caller 2: Sir I can assure you we are Card Services.

Me: I don't think so...you're not really good at it.

Caller 2: And how much have you made today?

Me: How much as in how much did I scam people of their money from being a phony call center disguised as a credit card service?

Caller 2: Yes.

Me: Gotcha.

<They hang up>

ANOTHER CREDIT CARD SCAMMER GETS THEIR TIME WASTED BY ME AGAIN

Caller: Hi Sir I see you pressed 1 and are responding to the offer to lower your credit card interest is that correct.

Me: Of course.

Caller: Well, I see in our records that you live in New Jersey.

Me: If you say so.

Caller: How much would you say is outstanding on your credit cards?

Me: Is that not in your records?

Caller: Sir, in order for us to help you we need to get an idea of how much you owe.

Me:(Incoherent mumbling, no actual number given)

Caller: Wow Sir, $50 thousand dollars. And how many cards is that from?

Me: One.

Caller: One card Sir, wow that's impressive.

Me: If you say so.

Caller: Is that a Visa or MasterCard?

Me: American Express Black Card

Caller: Sir just to clarify, you have $50,000 on your Amex Black Card

Me: And?

<At this point I could tell this person was giddy that they found a sucker to scam.>

Caller: Sir, can you tell me how much you pay monthly on your Amex Black Card?

Me: Probably more than you make a month.

Caller: Sir, can you tell me what percentage interest you pay?

Me: No idea, I just pay the bill every month

Caller: Sir, can you read the last 4 digits of the card to me so we can match it with your records?

Me: I can't!

Caller: Why?

Me: Because it's a new digitally encrypted card that displays no numbers

Caller: Sir, I never heard of such a thing.

Me: You haven't? Wow, you think you would, considering you're a scammer and I just wasted your time.

NOTE: Most scammers only need the last 4 digits of your credit card number along with the expiration date and billing zip code to cross match if the card is active. And when the card doesn't match they ask for the full card number and the toll free number on the back of the card. These scammers know if they contact the credit card issuer they have a better chance of making sure your card has funds for them to steal.

This Is Not A Solicitation Call!

We have been monitoring your credit cards for the last six months and can offer you a lower interest rate than what you are currently paying. Press #1 to speak to one of our experienced team members who will share with you how this {scam} works.

Call taker: Sir, I see you pressed 1 for a lower interest rate, before we continue can you tell me the expiration date of the highest balance card you have?

Me: Where are you located?

Call taker: Georgia, Atlanta Georgia.

Me: Oh and you are just randomly calling people?

Call taker: No Sir, we are working with Experian to offer their customers an opportunity to lower their credit card interest rates.

Me: Hmm, why is Experian giving out my information?

Call taker: Sir, {caller raises voice} WE HAVE ALL YOUR INFORMATION ON FILE WE JUST NEED YOU TO RECONFIRM

Me: Why?

Call taker: Sir, we want to give you the best rate possible. Now please read the toll free number on back of the card.

Me: Hang on...need to put my glasses on.

Call taker: Okay Sir, take your time.

Me: I put my bifocals on, but the print is too small I can't see the toll free number.

Call taker: Okay Sir, can you read the entire 16 digits on the card to me?

Me: Since you already have confirmed that you have my information, then why do I need to read off the entire 16 digits of the card?

Call taker: It's for your security Sir.

Me: Huh, you would think if it was for my security, you would have asked my name at the beginning of the call to make sure I was actually the right person.

Call taker: bhenchod {Indian and Pakistani slang for...well just look it...it's not nice}

Me: Oh, so you're not in Atlanta Georgia then...mostly likely Pakistan.

Call taker hangs up.

Rob Anspach

Press 1 to be Connected to Our Idiot Scammers Who Don't Stay On Script.

Scammer: Sir I see you pressed 1 to lower your interest rate.

Me: Well I did press 1 but it didn't seem to do anything, so I pressed 2, then 4, then 8, then 9, then the pound sign, then the asterisk symbol...and then you answered the call.

Scammer: Well Sir do you want to lower your rate or not.

Me: You're kind of pushy.

Scammer: I don't know what you said.

Me: Yes, I want to lower my interest.

Scammer: What cards do you have?

Me: I have baseball cards, business cards, index cards and some credit cards which one's interest you?

Scammer: Sir, do you have a Visa, MasterCard, Discover and American Express card

Me: Go Fish.

Scammer: What you say?

Me: Hey where are you located?

Scammer: Why do you ask stupid questions?

Me: I see you don't know how to stay on the script, I don't think you're cut out for this job.

Scammer: I'm your father.

Me: Oh, yeah that's great line, but my name isn't Luke Skywalker and you're no Darth Vader.

Scammer: F-you.

Me: So no lower interest rate then?

{He hung up}

NOTE: The moment you distract these scammers and they start to ad-lib and not follow the script is when they slip up. Unfortunately, once they get off script they usually end the call.

Press 1 To Be Connected To Card Services

Caller: Sir, I see you pressed 1 to lower your rate.

Me: I don't know who you are. I don't know what you want. If you are looking for my credit card information, I can tell you I don't have any. But what I do have are a very particular set of skills, skills I have acquired over a very long career. Skills that make me a nightmare for people like you. If you stop calling now, that'll be the end of it. I will not look for you, I will not pursue you. But if you don't, I will record you, I will make fun of you, and I will waste your time.

Caller hung up

I was surprised the caller actually waited until I was done saying all that before he hung up.

Although not more than 3 minutes later I was called again, by the same number. This time a different person answered, but hung up after I said "I don't know who you are."

NOTE: Don't be surprised if you get multiple calls on the same day by the same scam center using the same caller ID number. They can be relentless. Fight back by using Hiya or Nomorobo to block these scammers.

This is Card Services - did you press 1 to lower your rate?

Me: Why is your caller ID coming up as Russia?

Card Services Rep: Russia? Your phone must be giving you an error.

Me: But I can hear people in the background speaking Russian.

Card Services Rep: Sir, there is no one here speaking Russian.

Me: Did you just wave your hand while you said that?

Card Services Rep: Sir, I have no idea what you mean.

Me: You did it again.

Card Services Rep: Sir, I have no idea what you are talking about.

Me: You just Obi Wan Kenobi'd me didn't you?

Card Services Rep: Sir, do want a lower interest rate or not?

Me: What do you need from me?

Card Services Rep: What is your card with the highest balance?

Me: As in how much I owe or the one with the highest award points?

Card Services Rep: Sir, can you read off the numbers please.

Me: Which card?

Card Services Rep: The highest balance.

{I make up 16 numbers)

Card Services Rep: Okay now the expiration date.

{I gave them a wrong date}

{Card Services rep reads all the numbers back to me. I say yup.}

Card Services Rep: Sir, are you sure those numbers are the right numbers?

Me: Yup, pretty sure.

Card Services Rep: Sir, the numbers you gave me don't match what we have on file. Is this your card?

Me: Yup.

Card Services Rep: Sir when was the last time you used this card?

Me: Why?

Card Services Rep: Our records show the card was cancelled 5 years ago.

Me: Really? It worked!

Card Services Rep: What worked?

Me: What year is it?

Card Services Rep: Sir it's 2018.

Me: 2018? 2018! I just went 6 years into the future. Yeehaw!

Card Services Rep: Sir, are you wasting my time?

Me: Time is relative I always say, especially if you have a time machine and love messing with scammers.

(caller hung up)

NOTE: If you receive a call and the voices you hear in the background speak multiple languages its usually a good indication it's a scam call center trying to steal your credit card information.

Don't hang up this is not a solicitation call. We are starving scam artists just trying to make a living.

Press 1 to be scammed.
{Me pressing 1}

Caller: Sir I see you pressed 1 to get a lower interest rate.

Me: Wow, you're good. You must have super powers or something to know what number I pressed.

Caller: How much do you owe on your credit cards.

Me: Wow, okay don't waste any time...you're in serious mode I get it.

Caller: Sir, do you want to lower your interest rate?

Me: Lower it by how much?

Caller: We can offer you as low as zero percent.

Me: Hmm...tell me about that "as low as" part.

Caller: Sir I can't give you specifics until you tell me which card has the highest balance.

Me: Well, they are all kind of high.

Caller: Okay let's start off with your Visa.

Me: Does it have to be a Visa first?

Caller: Okay we can start off with your MasterCard then.

Me: How about Discover?

Caller: Yes, yes, we can do that one too.

Me: How about Diners Card?

Caller: Sir just give me one of the numbers, I don't care which one?

Me: Okay, 3.

Caller: 3 what?

Me: You said you just needed one of the numbers.

Caller: Sir I need the whole 16-digit card number

Me: So why didn't you say that instead of saying give me one of the numbers?

Caller: Sir you are wasting my time.

Me: Am I?

Caller: If you aren't going to give me the information I need then, yes, you are wasting my time.

Me: You called me, how am I wasting your time?

Caller: Sir, give me one of your card numbers or I'm hanging up.

Me: 5

{He hung up}

NOTE: In most cases if you were to call your credit card company and ask questions they would never accuse you of wasting their time. It's their job to make sure you are satisfied with the call. A scammer will rush the call and get angry when you don't cooperate. And unfortunately, when a call starts off with "this is not a solicitation call" it's usually a clear sign to hang up right then and there, because it's a scam.

Rob Versus The Scammers

CHAPTER 7

Do You Accept Credit Cards?

Sadly, many entrepreneurs fall for this scam.

Do You Accept Credit Cards?

I want to know if you're a sucker and fall for scams?

Well the text I received didn't actually start off that way, but it quickly escalated to that point.

You see these scams start out by seeing if you offer a particular service and if you accept credit cards.

This is the text I received the other night...

"I'm David and I want to know if you can build an informational website design for my new company and do you accept credit card payments?"

I respond, "YES"

To which I received...

"Thank you I have a small clothing business for both male and female, now am trying to expand the business and I want you to build an informational website for it for advertisement and to increase my sales rate. The site would only be informational, so I need you to get back to me with an estimate for the web design, the estimate should include hosting and I want the site to have not more than 15 pages since it is informational. I have a private project graphic designer, he has the text content, images and the logos for the site.

Note:

1. I want only English language

2. I don't have a domain yet but I want the domain name as Travis Fashion's House

3. You will be updating the site for me.

4. I will be proving the images, logos and content for the site.

5. I want the site up and running before ending of next month.

Kindly get back to me with an estimate."

I thought weird, but okay.

So I respond, "David what is your last name and where are you located?"

He responds, "Allan David Lancaster PA, kindly get back to me with an estimate so I know my budget"

Hmm, I thought that is very close to where I live.

So I dug deeper with my questioning and I asked, "How did you hear about our services?"

No immediate response.

I thought yup, a scam and I was going to leave it at that.

Then 3 hours later he responds, "I got your info on bbb.org with a good recommendation. So what will be the cost?"

I respond with, "Really, didn't know we had a listing on the BBB."

Not less than 5 seconds later he responds with "OK"

Then asks again "So what is the total cost so I know my budgets??"

A minute goes by and he sends another text... "you there?"

I respond, "what's your mailing address?"

He sends me an address that is real and about 10 minutes away.

I quickly do a Google search on that address, he's not listed.

I ask him if that is where his web store will be located.

He says, "yes and kindly get back to me with an estimate"

Well at this point I had also reached out to one of my team members and he reaffirmed that it's a scam and sent me a copy of a text he had just received...

"Greetings my name is Ken Nelson, I need to know if you can handle a website design for a new company and do you take credit cards for payments?"

Although Ken's text was a bit of a variation on David's

"Thanks for the response back, I will like to speak with you through the phone but actually i am an hearing impaired that is why i contacted you via mail, I have small scale business which I want to turn into large scale business now it located in and the company is based on importing and exporting of Agriculture products such as Kola Nut, Gacillia Nut and Cocoa so i need a best of the best layout design for it. Can you handle that for me? So I need you to check out this site but I need something more perfect than this if it's possible the site would only be informational, so I need you to give me an estimate based on the site i gave you to check out, the estimate should include hosting and i want the same page as the site i gave you to check out and i have a private project consultant, he has the text content and the logos for the site."

So knowing that it's a full out right scam we (my team and I) decided to play along with David and see how far it would go.

I reply to David...

"Well I spoke to my team and a 15-page website is just too small for our busy schedule. However, for $20k I bet I can convince them to work with you."

Under 20 seconds and David comes back with "Ok thanks very much"

Then he proceeds to lay out his scam...

"I will like to make an upfront payment of $3,000 for the web design and do you accept credit cards for payment? Also I will be needing a little assistance from you"

I respond, "Assistance?"

David gives a big YES reply.

I say, "What assistance do you need?"

Then he spells out his ploy...

"I understand the content for this site would be needed so as for the job to commence so regarding the content I will need a Little favor from you and the reason I need this favor from you is because the project consultant does not have the facility to charge credit cards and i will be glad if you can help me out with this favor,

{5 second pause in-between texts}

I would give you my card info's to charge for $8,000, so $3,000 would be a deposit payment for my website design and the remaining $5,000 you would help me send it to the project consultant that has the text content and the logo for my website so once he has the $5000 he would send the text content and logo needed for my website to you also the funds would be sent to him via Bank transfer into his account, sending of funds would be after funds clears into your account and also $50 tip for you stress. So I will be looking forward to read back from you."

Hah, David thinks he slick so I up the ante on him a bit and reply...

"Well since our service is $20k and you want us to give your consultant $5k we will need to add a 20% surcharge to cover your guy. So the price will be $30,000"

And he responds, "Alright I will send you my credit card information to charge thru $10,000 first and then after it clears we can proceed with the balance is that okay?"

So I respond, "I will need card number, expiration date, CVV number, name on card, billing address, zip code and phone number."

Five minutes later I get from David..."Ok good, but before I provide you the info I will like to know what merchant you use in processing my credit card?

I send "WHY?

David quickly replies, "I ask because my card don't work with Square and PayPal. I won't go through."

I respond sarcastically, "that's sad"

David's responds with "what's wrong"

I say, "I never heard of Square or PayPal not letting cards go thru."

He informs me that he's tried using them and both gave him problems.

He asks, "What merchant are you using to charge my card?"

I say I have several.

David sends...

"Ok which one are you willing to use so I can inform my bank to avoid delay transaction. And how many days those it take funds to clear into your account?"

"Kindly let me know"

I respond again with "send me the info and I'll process"

I receive, "Okay hold"

Ten minutes go by and I respond...

"What am I holding for?"

David responds with "my card information"

And at this point it's about 10pm my time and I wanted to see if I could trip him up so I ask him..."what time is it there?"

The idiot texts "7pm"

So now I know he's (1) not local to me at all and (2) with a 3-hour time difference he's probably on the West Coast somewhere or (3) has no clue what time zone I really am in.

So now I press deeper...

"Do you have the information yet?"

Then he does something that really surprised me!

He sent me a card number with a CVV #, an expiration date and a zip code.

The zip code was 34473 which is Marion Oaks Florida. And remember he told me he was initially located about 10 minutes away from me.

I ask him for the name on the card and a billing address.

20 minutes go by and nothing.

Well the first 4 digits of the credit card indicate it's from Chase - so I call them.

As a merchant you can call any credit card company and verify funds availability.

The Chase rep informed me the card was valid, but since I had a feeling it was in the hands of a scammer I told the rep the whole story.

The rep thanked me and placed the card on the fraud list and locked the card.

Just as I was getting off the phone with Chase, David the scammer was texting me a new card number.

This one was issued to Citi and David included an address that was from New Rochelle NY and he says, "Charge my business master card instead."

I reply, "Your first card has been locked and marked as fraudulent, what gives? I'm calling the second card directly to see if funds are available."

David responds with, "You probably entered the numbers incorrectly, try again."

Then he adds, "Process the second card I gave you and please enter the numbers correctly."

{2 minutes go by}

David texts, "Did you charge it through yet?"

I reply, "Both cards are stolen what are you trying to pull?"

Then David asks if I have a Clover Merchant account.

I don't respond for about 10 minutes.

David asks "Are you there?"

So I say, "Are you there"

David then follows up with...
"It's late now, I suggest we proceed tomorrow so I can confirm what's going on maybe it's from my end most likely you entered numbers wrong. Is that clear?"

I reply, "Nope, I think I'm done playing your game."

He wonders what game.

I say, "Giving me 2 stolen credit cards. Telling me your address is close by yet your credit cards are from Florida and New York and when I ask you what time it is - you told me a time that puts you on the West Coast. Plus, you are texting me from a spoofed number."

David texts, "Am a business man and I travel around the state am so sorry for the inconvenience. That why I need to call my bank and know what's going on I promise by tomorrow you will have the payment on my credit card. I will give you my wife card to charge."

I reply..."No Thank You. We Are Done!"

Well apparently we weren't done.

As the very next day I started getting texts from this scammer again.

"I want you to believe me with this I spoke with my bank rep and told me my card is cancelled already that why it's was reported stolen I guess."

So I reply... "What's the name of your bank."

He sends..."BOA" (which stands for Bank of America)

I then ask for his email address.

He sends - allandavid6066@gmail.com

Then he asks, "Can I send you another card to proceed now?"

I reply, "Is your name on the card?"

"YES", he sends back

So I tell him to take a picture of the card (front & back) and send to me.

I get, "My cam is bad. I can only text you the necessary info to charge."

{a minute goes by}

And we are back to the same question as yesterday.

"What merchant are you using to charge my card?"

So I send him, "After 2 bad cards, I need proof. Send a picture of the card front and back"

Then I get from him, "I told you my card was cancelled. I guess that's why it was reported stolen and that's why I need to know what merchant you are using to charge my card. My cam is not working fine."

I zip off, "Well find a way to take a photo of it. I need proof."

Then no word for almost 12 hours.

David sends me, "I don't have a good phone to snap a card. Like I said I am on a business trip with my colleague here. Please just let me text you the card info and am very sure it will go through. I need the website in no time."

So I reply, "Have your colleague snap the picture. I can't process it without proof."

Then I receive…

"I don't want him to know about the payment I want to make because he's asking me to lend him some money with me and explained to him I have a lot to do with the money left with me and if am asking him to lend me his phone to snap he would know. Please try and understand me and trust me you will have all the funds charge on my card. You have nothing to worry about because I have already been to my bank today to let them know my card was reported stolen and told me it was cancelled. It's happened because it's a joint account me and my wife and we are having a little misunderstanding with her so she went ahead cancelling the card. Kindly bear with me and am sorry for inconvenience. God bless you."

David then asks, "Are you there with me?"

I respond, "I'll need a picture of your driver's license too."

I receive back, "That's no problem I can send it along with my card information."

Days go by and no reply.

And I'm still waiting...

Rob Versus The Scammers

Rob Anspach

CHAPTER 8

Microsoft Warning Scam

Whatever you do, don't call the number displayed!

Have you received a blue Microsoft Warning Alert message?

Maybe after landing on the wrong URL or being diverted to a page after clicking on what you thought was the right URL.

Hey it happens.

These deplorable scam artists embed these descriptive messages into URL's in hopes of getting you to shell out your hard earned dollars.

They try to create fear with the words they use...
DO NOT IGNORE THIS CRITICAL ALERT.
IF YOU CLOSE THIS PAGE, YOUR COMPUTER ACCESS WITH BE DISABLED TO PREVENT FURTHER DAMAGE TO OUR NETWORK.

Then they try to increase that fear level by saying your information is being captured such as your...
•   Facebook logins
•   Credit Card Details
•   Email Account Logins
•   Photos stored on your computer

None of this is true...unless you call the number on the screen.

Once you initiate a call, they will try to assure you that they are there to help and everything will be okay.
Since your guard is down, and you believe they will help, they will ask you to download or grant access to a screen

sharing software.

Then they will show you codes or programs that you didn't even know about...most are legit, and some are actually there to prevent intrusions.

Once access is granted...it's a free for all for the scammers.

They have your computer, your information, your credit card and sadly they haven't fixed a darn thing.

For MAC users it's a simple click the red "exit page" button and the warning goes away.

Unfortunately, for PC users, it can become an all day ordeal (less if you know what you are doing) scanning your system, checking for viruses and cleaning out rogue programs.

But never ever call the number displayed on the screen. **It's a scam.**

They will make your computer worse, copy your information and take your money.

Don't fall for it.

Rob Versus The Scammers

CHAPTER 9

Craigslist Auto Sales Scam

If they want payment before letting you see the car…it's a scam.

Car For Sale...Or Is It?

Trust starts with being honest, not a deception.
Some websites are filled with scams and otherwise
dubious ways to maliciously harm people.

The buy and sell sites are notoriously rampant with these
scams.

Recently, I was looking up used cars on Craigslist and
discovered a massive scam going on.

Listing…

*I am glad you are one of the people interested in buying
my car. It is a 2005 Chevrolet Equinox. Red color/ gray
cloth interior with only 61,990 mileage. Automatic
transmission. The price is $2000.*

*The car is a non-smoker and interior is in great shape.
All power components work absolutely perfect. All
regular maintenance has been performed on this car. The
tires are in great condition, and the brakes work well.
Has never been in an accident and needs nothing at this
time. This car truly should go to someone that will
appreciate a car in EXCELLENT condition that look as
good as it. Because of my divorce settlement, I own this
car and as a woman I don't need it so I'm trying to get
rid of it as soon as possible. The title is legally under my
name, clear and free of any liens or loans.*

Please let me know if you are interested and where are

you located.

Thank you,
Susan
Local # to text

The scammer posts a car in hopes of luring people in. They list a local number to text. If you are the one looking for a vehicle you send a text message then get a reply saying to email the person's mother at susanlopez996@gmail.com. Then you email the person and lo and behold the story posted online seems to have changed and the person now wants you to send payment before you will even get the car.

I discovered the below email has been used in multiple scams across the US.

***Here's the email I received from susanlopez996@gmail.com ***

"I'm a flight attendant for American Airlines and because I'm away most of the time I will not be able to deal in person. Before leaving I had pre-arranged a deal with eBay so my presence is not necessary. The vehicle is in their possession ready to be delivered. eBay will handle this transaction for me. The total amount that you will pay is $2000, with shipping and transfer fees included. You will receive the vehicle in max 48 hours and you will have the chance to inspect it for 5 days. The eBay department will hold and insure your money throughout the inspection. If by any reason you find something you don't like about the car you can send it back at my expense and eBay will send you a full refund.

I'm sure it won't be the case because the vehicle is in excellent condition. It will come with all the necessary paperwork (clear title, bill of sale, user's manual etc). You will receive all the original documents. I signed all the paperwork and the clear title is ready to be transferred to the new owner. If you are interested in buying my vehicle please send me your full name, shipping address and phone number so I can register the transaction with eBay and they will reply you with more details and information about this transaction."

NOTE: The email associated with this Susan Lopez has a long line of scams associated with it and seems to go back years on Google. Searches have pulled up scam after scam after scam.

CHAPTER 10

Coca Cola Lottery Scam

If I had a dollar for every random email saying I won.

You Won $10,000,000.00

Dear Esteemed Winner,

Your email has won you $10,000,000.00 (Ten Million US Dollars) in the Coca-Cola Worldwide 2018 promotions.

Your email was selected in our random Computer draw of valid emails sponsored by the Coca-Cola Company, Microsoft, and Hotmail. Yahoo, Gmail and other email Domain.

Your email address emerged as the Jackpot winner, winning you a Total Sum of Ten Million United States dollars with Your Payment Code: SA209 Forward the required details:
Name:
Age:
Sex:
Occupation:
Country of Origin/Residence:
Telephone Number:

To our email: cocacola.promotions@op.pl
For your Payment Instruction.
Congratulations
John Chao

*Coca-Cola, nor Microsoft, Hotmail, Yahoo or Gmail operate email lotteries. Nor do they use a .pl email.

CHAPTER 11

Bitcoin Email Scams

This one has caught many off guard, and some have paid. It may sound ominous, but it's not. Don't fall for it.

Bitcoin Email Scam #1

Hello!
I'm a programmer who cracked your email account and device about half year ago.

You entered a password on one of the insecure site you visited, and I catched it.

Your password from [lists a very old password] on moment of crack: [lists the very old password again]

Of course you can will change your password, or already made it. But it doesn't matter, my rat software update it every time.

Please don't try to contact me or find me, it is impossible, since I sent you an email from your email account.

Through your e-mail, I uploaded malicious code to your Operation System.

I saved all of your contacts with friends, colleagues, relatives and a complete history of visits to the Internet resources.

Also I installed a rat software on your device and long tome spying for you.

You are not my only victim, I usually lock devices and ask for a ransom.

But I was struck by the sites of intimate content that you very often visit.

I am in shock of your reach fantasies! Wow! I've never seen anything like this!

I did not even know that SUCH content could be so exciting!

So, when you had fun on intimate sites (you know what I mean!)

I made screenshot with using my program from your camera of yours device.

After that, I jointed them to the content of the currently viewed site.

Will be funny when I send these photos to your contacts! And if your relatives see it?

BUT I'm sure you don't want it. I definitely would not want to ...

I will not do this if you pay me a little amount.
I think $820 is a nice price for it!

I accept only Bitcoins.
My BTC wallet: {lists a 34-digit code}

If you have difficulty with this - Ask Google "how to make a payment on a bitcoin wallet". It's easy.

After receiving the above amount, all your data will be immediately removed automatically.

My virus will also will be destroy itself from your operating system. My Trojan have auto alert, after this email is looked, I will be know it!

You have 2 days (48 hours) for make a payment.

If this does not happen - all your contacts will get crazy shots with your dirty life!

And so that you do not obstruct me, your device will be locked (also after 48 hours)

Do not take this frivolously! This is the last warning!

Various security services or antiviruses won't help you for sure (I have already collected all your data).

Here are the recommendations of a professional: Antiviruses do not help against modern malicious code.

Just do not enter your passwords on unsafe sites!

I hope you will be prudent.
Bye.

Bitcoin Email Scam #2

You can complain to the cops but they can't help you.

I am foreigner.

It means nobody can track my location even for 6 months. Your system was infected by our malicious soft.

We had access to your webcam.

During RDP session I downloaded your contact list so if you want me to stay silent you must pay 430 USD in bitcoins.

Use this bitcoin address for payment
{lists a 34-digit code}
(use it like your credit card number)

You have 30 hours after clicking on this message for making the transaction. There is no need to tell me that you have paid.

This bitcoin wallet was given only to you, everything will be removed automatically after transfer verification.

You can get 48 h only reply on this letter with +. Bye.

Think about the shame.

Bitcoin Scam Email #3

Hello!

I have very bad news for you.
03/08/2018 - on this day I hacked your OS and got full access to your account {lists my email address}

On this day your account {lists my email address again} has password: {lists a very old password}

So, you can change the password, yes.. But my malware intercepts it every time.

How I made it:
In the software of the router, through which you went online, was a vulnerability.
I just hacked this router and placed my malicious code on it.
When you went online, my trojan was installed on the OS of your device.

After that, I made a full dump of your disk (I have all your address book, history of viewing sites, all files, phone numbers and addresses of all your contacts).

A month ago, I wanted to lock your device and ask for a not big amount of btc to unlock.
But I looked at the sites that you regularly visit, and I was shocked by what I saw!!!
I'm talk you about sites for adults.

I want to say - you are a BIG pervert. Your fantasy is

shifted far away from the normal course!

And I got an idea....
I made a screenshot of the adult sites where you have fun
(do you understand what it is about, huh?).
After that, I made a screenshot of your joys (using the
camera of your device) and glued them together.
Turned out amazing! You are so spectacular!

I'm know that you would not like to show these
screenshots to your friends, relatives or colleagues.
I think $837 is a very, very small amount for my silence.
Besides, I have been spying on you for so long, having
spent a lot of time!

Pay ONLY in Bitcoins!
My BTC wallet: {lists a 34 digit code}

You do not know how to use bitcoins?
Enter a query in any search engine: "how to replenish btc
wallet".
It's extremely easy

For this payment I give you a little over two days
(exactly 55 hours).
As soon as this letter is opened, the timer will work.

After payment, my virus and dirty screenshots with your
enjoys will be self-destruct automatically.
If I do not receive from you the specified amount, then
your device will be locked, and all your contacts will
receive a screenshots with your "enjoys".

I hope you understand your situation.

- Do not try to find and destroy my virus! (All your data, files and screenshots is already uploaded to a remote server)
- Do not try to contact me (you yourself will see that this is impossible, I sent this email from your account)
- Various security services will not help you; formatting a disk or destroying a device will not help, since your data is already on a remote server.

P.S. You are not my single victim. so, I guarantee you that I will not disturb you again after payment!
 This is the word of honor hacker

I also ask you to regularly update your antiviruses in the future. This way you will no longer fall into a similar situation.

Do not hold evil! I just do my job.
Good luck.

NOTE: If you get an email similar to the ones listed above, don't panic. In most cases the information they obtained regarding passwords or usernames is very old (in my case about 6 years old). They really don't have anything current on you. And unfortunately, there is no way once payment is made by bitcoin to reverse it. Don't reply to their email, just delete it.

CHAPTER 12

Foreigners Bearing Gifts

These scams have been around since the dawn of the internet and yet, people still fall for them.

The Ole' "Next Of Kin" Scam

My name is Mr. Owen Botes, I work with a private security and deposit firm in United Kingdom. With my position as the General Manager of this firm, I am privileged to classified information on client's records. Over the last few years I have been monitoring one particular deposit account owned by an American businessman who died since 2008 with no details of any next of kin.

I am looking for a trust-worthy foreign partner with whom I can work with and present as next of Kin for this account in order to claim this deposit and I am willing to share these funds 50/50 with this individual. I will be retiring from this company by next year and there is no better time to pull this deal than now.

I have over the years worked-out a perfect modality to successfully claim this fund, by whoever I present as a next of kin to this deceased client irrespective of his or her country of origin.

Kindly get back to me if you are interested in this deal so that I can provide you with more information's on how we can execute this.

Waiting your urgent response
Mr. Owen Botes

*There is no next of kin, but I'm sure there will be fees involved that Mr. Botes wants up front from you.

This Partnership Won't End Well

DAVID LOUIS SOLICITORS AND ASSOCIATES
3 Whitmore Gardens
London, NW10 5HH
Tel: +44-770-030-9075

Dear Friend,

RE: MUTUAL PARTNERSHIP

I am David Louis, a British citizen and also the personal attorney to one Robert Fitzpatrick, an American who was a consultant with Shell UK LTD here in London, who shall be referred to as my client. Unfortunately my client lost his life on Boeing Egypt Air Flight 990, which crashed into the Atlantic Ocean on October 31st, 1999 and left no clear beneficiary as Next of Kin except some vital documents related to the deposit still with me.

All efforts by me to trace his Next of Kin proved abortive because he did not make any will prior to his death. Since then I have made several inquiries to locate any of my late clients extended relatives and this has proved unsuccessful. After my several unsuccessful attempts to locate any member of his family hence I contacted you.

My intention of contacting you is to assist in claiming the money left behind by my client before they get confiscated or in other words seized or declared unclaimed by the security company where this huge deposit was deposited. Particularly, the finance company where the deceased had the said fund valued at

US$11,000,000.00 (Eleven Million United State Dollars) has issued me a notice to provide the next of kin.

Consequent upon this, my idea is that we can have a deal/agreement and I am going to do this legally with your name as the bonafide beneficiary of the amount in question as I have all legal document to back our claim, I seek your consent to present you as the next of kin to the deceased so that the proceeds of this account valued at $11 Million US dollars can be paid to your account abroad, note that 40% of this money will be for you, in respect to the provision of a foreign account and 50% for me, 10% will be used for the reimbursement of any expenditure we may incur in the cause of the transaction.

I guarantee that this will be executed under a legitimate arrangement that will protect you from any breach of the law, all I need from you is your utmost collaboration and sincerity for us to thrive in this deal. Get back to me ASAP for further advise if you are interested in this proposed partnership. However, if you are not interested please do keep me informed as well so I can proceed further with my search.

Looking forward to your urgent response.
Yours Sincerely,
David Louis.

*This scam has been around since the dawn of the internet. Yet, good people fall for it. Don't let it be you.

Good Samaritan Scam

I greet you with the name of our Lord Jesus Christ; it is true that this letter may come to you as a surprise. Nevertheless, I humbly ask you to give me your attention and hear me well.

My name is Mrs. Patricia Anderson. From Zimbabwe. I was brought up from a motherless baby's Home in Harare Zimbabwe in my Country and was married to my late husband Dr. Johan Anderson, who are a farmer in Zimbabwe I'm here in South Africa I live Here Now Because Of The Problem We Have in Zimbabwe With Zimbabwe Former President Robert Mugabe About land Reform, for a period of 7years before my husband died. We were married for 20 Years without a child before he died in a fatal car accident. Since his death I decided not to Remarry due to my religious belief .I am 59 years old, and am suffering from a long time cancer of the breast which also affected my brain from all indication my conditions is really deteriorating And it is quite obvious that, according to my doctors they have advised me that I may not live for The next three months this is because the cancer stage has gotten to a very bad stage

When my late husband was alive he deposited the sum of US$6,000,000.00 (Six Million United State American Dollars) with a Bank here in South Africa. Presently this Money is still in the custody of the Bank in South Africa. Recently, my Doctor told me that I would not last for the next three months due to cancer illness.
HAVING KNOWN MY CONDITION I DECIDED TO DONATE THIS MONEY TO CHURCHES,

ORGANIZATIONS OR GOOD PERSON THAT WILL UTILIZE THIS MONEY THE WAY I AM GOING TO INSTRUCT HEREIN.

I want you to use this money for (Churches, Charity organizations), orphanages, widows and other people that are in need. l took this decision because I don't have any child that will inherit this Money. Moreover, my husband relatives are not close to me since I develop a Cancer problem and it had been their wish to see me dead in order to inherit his wealth since we have no Child. These people are not worthy of this inheritance. This is why I am taking this decision.

I don't need any telephone communication in this regard because of my ill-health. As soon as I Receive your reply I will give you the contact of the Bank where this money is deposited and I WILL ALSO ISSUE A LETTER OF AUTHORIZATION TO THE BANK THAT WILL PROVE YOU THE PRESENT BENEFICIARY OF THIS MONEY. I ALSO WANT YOU TO ALWAYS PUT ME IN PRAYER.

THE TOTAL FUNDS TO BE TRANSFERRED TO YOU ARE US$6,000,000.00 (SIX MILLION UNITED STATE AMERICAN DOLLARS.) IN WHICH 50% WILL BE YOURS AND 50% WILL BE FOR THE LESS PRIVILEGED AND THE HOMELESS PEOPLE IN THE SOCIETY.

MEANWHILE L WILL LIKE YOU TO SEND ME SOME OF YOUR INFORMATION LIKE YOUR FULL NAME, NATIONALITY, OCCUPATION, AGE, AND RELIGION TO ENABLE MY ATTORNEY TO WRITE

OUT AN AUTHORIZATION LETTER ON MY
BEHALF AND TO THE BANK AND INSTRUCT
THEM TO MAKE THE MONEY AVAILABLE TO
YOU SO THAT THE BANK WILL GIVE YOU THE
MONEY ON MY BEHALF. L WILL ALSO
FORWARD TO YOU THE AUTHORIZATION
LETTER AS A PROVE TO YOU. AND YOU MAY
VIEW MY RECENT IN THE HOSPITAL,

Please Reply To Me At My Email Address At
: mrs.patricia2017@gmail.com

Any delay in your reply may give me room to look for
another good person for this same purpose. Please assure
me that you will act accordingly as I stated herein.

Thanks and Remain Blessed,

Yours Sister in The Lord,

Mrs. Patricia Anderson

***Yup, the "use religion to soften the heart" ploy
combined with the offer to give away millions and it
turns nice folks into victims really quick.**

Rob Versus The Scammers

Rob Versus The Scammers

CHAPTER 13

Domain Jacking

It seems the moment you register a domain; these scammers start
swooping in like starving vultures.

That Cool Domain You Just Bought Is Now A Target.

Somebody with a deep Indian accent just called me from what sounded like "Frozen Salmon Technologies" about a domain I recently purchased for a client.

When I wouldn't give him "YES" or "NO" answers he got frustrated and hung up.

If you have recently purchased a new domain and a company you're not familiar with calls you inquiring about it, do not under any circumstances give out information or say "Yes or No".

These people will use your phone call as a way to take over your domain and hold it hostage forcing you to pay big bucks to get it back.

It seems to be prevalent for those buying domains through GoDaddy (due to their size as an industry leader in the domain selling space), but I have heard of lesser known domain companies being targeted as well.

The scammers ask you a few questions hoping you will say YES or NO and with those answers can generate a verbal authorization to the domain issuer (GoDaddy or similar) and quickly transfer your domain into their system.

Now instead of paying GoDaddy $12 a year for your domain you are forced to pay $100 or more to the scammers.

And trying to get your domain back can be worse than having a double root canal.

Be vigilant.

Don't let these scammers steal your domain.

If the caller isn't representing the exact service you bought the domain from...just hang up.

Rob Versus The Scammers

CHAPTER 14

Even More Scams

Yup, just click the link…what's the worst that could happen?

Random Strangers With Money

Hello

Are you frustrated by the lack of available funding options out there, or think you might not qualify? You'd be surprised by how many executives and owners I've helped just like you.

My company is the leading provider of alternative funding solutions in the United States, and we have the rates to prove it.

For you the process is simple, with a full service lending platform and a funding time of less than 24 hours.

May I give you more information? I look forward to hearing from you.

Thank you,
Josh

*Josh sounds so nice doesn't he...until he rips you off.

Update Your Password To Lose All Your Money

Hi

Your password has been recuperated effectively.

Your updated password is: ********

The following link will take you directly into your account:

Safe access to your account
{unsafe URL}

When you have logged in, you can quickly adjust your password on your account page.

Please do not think twice to contact us with any type of concerns.

To Your Success,
Green

* Of course it's safe, what could go wrong?

Lose Admin Rights To Your Facebook in 3...2...1

Hello

The deadline for Facebook Page admins to apply for messaging permissions is coming up. Facebook admins should apply before Dec. 31. Facebook application cheat sheet inside.

If you're a Page admin and this news sounds like it affects you, read on for everything you need to know about the change, how to apply, and tips for getting approved.

Be a Unicorn in a Sea of Donkeys!

Best,
Larry

*Yup, scammers love unicorns.

Ooh, Free Money...Nope!

Howdy

I intended to alert you that you have actually obtained an inbound payment and also the funds are accepted
Simply go here right away for more information

This was sent out the other day and also is currently accepted funds!

To Your Success,

Douglas

— — — — — — — — — — — — — — — — —

Hello
This is a certified email relating to the reversed pay out modification:
Just take a look at THIS: **Reversed Payout is Updated & Set (Visit This Site Currently)**

Best Regards,
Newman

*If you didn't request it, don't click on it.

Dolla Bills, Y'all

Hey,

Wake up, check how much money you have made, and go enjoy your time with your family with your pockets full.

Sounds OK?

Here's how:

GO HERE NOW>

Regards,
Jenna

— — — — — — — — — — — — — — — — —

Howdy

EEC pays regular on Sunday for the week finishing the day previously.
I have actually been paid $7,798 in EEC since May 19th
You could sign up with as well as make in any type of nation.
<<< **Sign up with as well as make free of charge!** >>>

Best wishes,

Jimenez

*Oh yeah, wake up to free money…makes sense, not!

Fake Jobs & Fast Money

Welcome to Fortune Steel and Gas Limited

Fortune Steel and Gas Ltd is urgently interested in your services and partnership. Get back to us for details on job description and compensation.

Thank you.

Sincerely,
Mr. Daniel Tatjung CHIU
Executive Director
Fortune Steel and Gas Limited

_ _ _ _ _ _ _ _ _ _ _ _ _ _ _ _ _ _ _

If you're done messing around and are looking for weekly paychecks, then stop and look at this.

Click Here: Once A Week Paychecks

Lots of people found this and started earning in as low as a few days, so please check this out and let me know what you think.

Click Here For Instant Access

Best,

*Just hand over your I.D. and the job is yours.

Website Development & SEO Scam

Hello there,

Looking to expand your business online? Do you want to increase your business outreach? Get a new website designed at a very minimal cost.

Services we provide:

1. Website development (Custom Website Development, PHP, Java, .Net Development, Ajax Programming, etc.)

2. Website designing (Logo Design, HTML designing, corporate website design, PSD to XHTML/HTML, etc.)

3. Internet Marketing (SEO, SMM, Reputation Management, PPC)

Interested!!

Share your contact details or simply reply back to this email and we will share the best possible price with you.

We will be waiting for your response :)

Neea
Business Development Executive

*Most of these services are out of India and Pakistan

Download Report Then Get Scammed

Hi,

Building an environment where employees have access to critical data, analysis, and experts in real-time and can quickly collaborate across any channel, improves daily productivity and long-term financial results.

Research from Aberdeen finds that businesses integrating communications across the entire company achieve 2.4 times greater revenue growth rate year-over-year. Unifying all internal and customer-facing departments under one common platform that combines phone, meetings, collaboration and contact center, empowers employees to innovate, respond and serve customers to deliver exceptional experiences.

Read the report to find out how unified communications helps:
- Drive data-driven decisions with real-time insights
- Deliver a seamless omni-channel customer experience
- Increase agent productivity and bottom line revenue

Download the full research report to learn more.
4th Floor, Viman Nagar, Pune Maharashtra, India

*Just delete the email, nothing good will come of it.

Top Secret Scam, Click The Link To Lose Big

Hey,

Did you check out this top secret Amazon system yet?

Everyone is talking about it and how it's making ordinary people up to $3,000 a day.

It's mind-blowing stuff!

Follow the simple instructions and you can earn $3K in the next 24 hours.

And then $15k within the next 5 days.

Click here to Sign Up

Regards,
Tim

*Never a last name, company name or phone number.

The "Crazy If You Miss This" Scam

"Your account is collecting"

All just by utilizing this innovative system (setup)

You now have the possibility to literally link into our system and setup autopilot commissions which run every day for you...

This gets the job done like clockwork...

Our registered members are recording every day revenues of 660 dollars each.

Would this help your loved ones?

You can get this paid directly to your financial account through wire OR setup a PayPal account.

You would be crazy to miss this possibility, I am personally using this myself.

It's amazing as I use this to pay off all my regular monthly payments, like rent, vehicle payments etc

=> Click on this hyperlink for direct access to setup

Let me know your everyday incomes after 1 week of utilization this, ok?

Kind regards,

Torres

* "Innovative system" is code for we are going to scam you.

This System Is So Effective...
At Scamming You!

Did you receive your wire payment today?

If not, then you must not have activated and setup the system: Activate here ASAP (confirm payments)

All members should have received their payments from last week's earnings from the system.

Great news as well, average member earnings were just under $2k each :-)

Those stats speak volumes about how effective this system is for our members.

Still not joined the system?

Look, if you are going to sit on the sidelines and keep missing these weekly payments then that is your choice, but...

Next week we will be earning again while you are reading next week's email.

It's super simple to setup...

>>> Click here to start getting paid weekly <<<

Let me know how much you earn by tomorrow, ok?

Best,

*The stats speak volumes...yeah, right.

CHAPTER 15

Avoiding & Reporting Scams

You'd better recognize!

Recognizing Scams

Most scams attempts involve one or more of the following:

- Email or text from someone that is not local to your area.

- Vague initial inquiry, e.g. asking about "the item." Poor grammar/spelling.

- Western Union, Money Gram, cashier check, money order, PayPal, shipping, escrow service, or a "guarantee."

- Inability or refusal to meet face-to-face to complete the transaction.

Phone scammers are notorious for spoofing local numbers to try to get you to answer the call. They will use the phone numbers of schools, hospitals and even local businesses to try to get you to pick up.

Using anti-scamming technology like Hiya or Nomorobo helps cut down on these nuisance calls.

How to Avoid Being Scammed

Deal locally, face-to-face —follow this one rule and avoid 99% of scam attempts.

If meeting locally or face-to-face isn't an option, then these extra tips should help...

1. Do not extend payment to anyone you have not met in person.
2. Beware offers involving shipping – deal with locals you can meet in person.
3. Never wire funds (example: Western Union) it's a notorious method for scammers.
4. Don't accept cashier/certified checks or money orders from people not local to your area or issued from a bank that you can't verify as legitimate.
5. Never pay for your high priced item in cash.
6. Transactions are between users only; no third party provides a "guarantee".
7. Never give out financial info (bank account, social security, PayPal account, etc).
8. Do not rent or purchase sight-unseen—that amazing "deal" may not exist.

Remember to always do your due diligence.

Reporting The Scammers

United States

Internet Fraud Complaint Center
FTC complaint form and hotline:
877-FTC-HELP (877-382-4357)

Consumer Sentinel/Military

https://www.militaryconsumer.gov/report-scam
(for Armed Service Members and Families)

Canada

Canadian Anti-Fraud Centre

http://www.antifraudcentre-centreantifraude.ca
or 888-495-8501 (toll-free)

Royal Canadian Mounted Police

http://www.rcmp-grc.gc.ca

United Kingdom

Action Fraud

National Fraud & Cyber Crime Reporting Centre
https://www.actionfraud.police.uk

If you are defrauded by someone you met in person, contact your local police department.

If you suspect that a Craigslist post may be connected to a scam, you can report directly to Craigslist.

Craigslist and EBay and other discount online websites work because they are advertised as a way for people to buy stuff cheaper than they would in a store. Sadly, scammers take advantage of people's need to save money. People clamor to these sites for the deals. Unfortunately, the deals in some cases are designed to take your money and leave you heartbroken and frustrated. Don't be a victim. Learn to report these scams if you see them. And warn your friends.

And if you get an email from a scammer with a disclaimer – all they are doing is trying to legitimize their scam.

Disclaimer: This email has been sent to the owner of email The CAN-SPAM Act of 2003 establishes requirements for those who send commercial email, spells out penalties for spammers and companies whose products are advertised in spam if they violate the law, and gives consumers the right to ask mailers to stop spamming them. The above mail is in accordance to the Can Spam act of 2003: There are no deceptive subject lines and is a manual process through our efforts on World Wide Web.

If you do not wish to receive any further communications of this type, send a reply **REMOVE**.

Do not reply...just delete the email.

OMG...

Some electric call scammer just called
me using the name
"Barry Allen"
So I reply...
*"Barry Allen as in **The FLASH**...
how fast you going to scam me out of
money?"*

The caller tells me to f-off and stop
answering his calls.

About The Author

Rob is an experienced Digital Marketing Strategist, Author, Corporate Ghostwriter, Speaker and Trust Creator who can transform and monetize your brand.

Rob has also produced books for many clients including lawyers, doctors, copywriters, speakers and consultants.

Rob helps companies across the globe generate new revenue and capture online business. And he hates scammers with a passion.

Rob is available to share talks and give interviews.

To learn more about Rob visit www.AnspachMedia.com or call Anspach Media at **(412)267-7224** today.

Other Books By Rob Anspach

Available on Amazon in Print & Kindle.

www.amazon.com/author/robertanspach

RESOURCES

TO PROTECT YOU AGAINST SCAMS

Hiya Call Block Security identifies the calls you want to take and blocks the numbers and texts you want to avoid. Hiya is free (no ads!), and is incredibly easy to use. Block calls, blacklist unwanted phone numbers and SMS text messages, reverse phone search incoming call information and receive spam alerts.

Download the free Hiya App at www.hiya.com
Available for Android & iOS

Nomorobo provides protection against robocalls and telemarketers. It's free on most major VoIP providers. And is available for iPhone and Android smartphones for a low monthly fee.

Visit www.nomorobo.com to get started.

Avast Free Antivirus raises the bar on security with real-time protection, intelligent threat-detection, and added security for your network, passwords, and browser. Easy to install and easy to use, no other free antivirus comes close.

Protect your computer today by visiting www.avast.com

Avast also provides protection against viruses, malware and phishing scams for your mobile devices.

If you have been scammed, defrauded or downright ripped off or wronged in anyway and need help, I highly recommend these fine people…

Private Investigators

Lisa Stensgard - www.YourEyeInvestigations.com

Dennis Eberly – www.OnTargetPIandConsultant.net

Michele Harris – www.HarrisInvestigations.net

Trademark & Copyright Attorney

(protecting your intellectual property rights)

Angela Langlotz – www.TrademarkDoctor.net

Law Enforcement

Call your local police and ask for the fraud or cyber department.

And Remember…

If The Offer Sounds Too Good To Be True…

It's Usually A Scam

Joe from Trip Advisor wants to give me a FREE Bahamas cruise. They just need me to confirm I am over 21 and have a credit card.

Apparently, Joe didn't even wait for me to say YES or NO - I was transferred to a live operator who wanted to know if I was now older than 25. And the cost would be $65 per person and the operator needed a commitment right now.

I said, *"Wow you work faster than Card Services at extracting money"*.

The phone operator says, *"Are you saying we're running a scam?"*

Me: Yup.

They hung up.

Guess I won't be going to the Bahamas anytime soon.

If You Would Like To Order Multiple Copies Of "Rob Versus The Scammers"

Visit

www.RobVersusTheScammers.com

You can also purchase the digital version on Amazon and give as a gift to your friends, colleagues and neighbors.

Just look for the "Buy for others" tab and gift away.

www.amazon.com/author/robertanspach

Remember to…

Share This Book!

Share it with your friends!

Share it with your colleagues!

Share it with law enforcement!

Share it on social media.

Share it using this hashtag...

#RobVersusTheScammers